spy, n. — a secret agent employed by a government or other organization to gather intelligence relating to its actual or potential enemies

Glove Pistol

Issued by U.S. Navy (ONI), circa 1942–1945

Armed with a glove pistol, an operative still had both hands free. To fire the pistol, the wearer pushed the plunger into an attacker's body.

Spies around the World

AND OTHER AMERICAN SPIES

Michael E. Goodman

CREATIVE
PAPERBACKS

A suspected member of a German spy ring is taken into custody by an FBI agent in 1941.

Table of Contents

Chapters

- -

Evolution of Espionage

- -

Published by Creative Paperbacks
P.O. Box 227, Mankato, Minnesota 56002
Creative Paperbacks is an imprint of
The Creative Company
www.thecreativecompany.us

Design and production by Blue Design
Art direction by Rita Marshall
Printed in the United States of America

Photographs by Alamy (67photo, AF archive, Everett
Collection Inc), Corbis (Bettmann, David Howells,
Hulton-Deutsch Collection), Flickr (The Central
Intelligence Agency), Getty Images (Boyer/Roger
Viollet, Peter C. Brandt, Fotosearch, Fox Photos,
Hulton Archive, Keystone, Keystone-France/Gamma-
Keystone, Greg Mathieson/Mai/Mai/Time Life Pictures,
Win Mcnamee/Department of Defense/Time Life Pictures,
MPI, New York Times Co., NY Daily News Archive,
Miami Herald/MCT, Paul Popper/Popperfoto, James L.
Stanfield/National Geographic, Bob Thomas/Popperfoto,
MIGUEL VINAS/AFP, Roger Viollet, Mark Wilson),
Library of Congress, Wikipedia (H. Seymour Squyer)

Library of Congress Cataloging-in-Publication Data
Goodman, Michael E.
The CIA and other American spies / by Michael E.
Goodman.
p. cm. — (Spies around the world)
Includes bibliographical references and index.
Summary: An eye-opening exploration of the history
of the 1942-founded CIA and other American espionage
agencies, investigating their typical training and
tools as well as the escapades of famous spies.
ISBN 978-1-60818-226-8 (hardcover)
ISBN 978-0-89812-969-4 (pbk)
1. Intelligence service—United States—Juvenile
literature. 2. United States. Central Intelligence
Agency—Juvenile literature. 3. Espionage, American—
Juvenile literature. 4. Spies—United States—Juvenile
literature. I. Title.

JK468.I6G664 2012
327.1273—dc23   2011035789

9 8 7 6 5 4 3 2

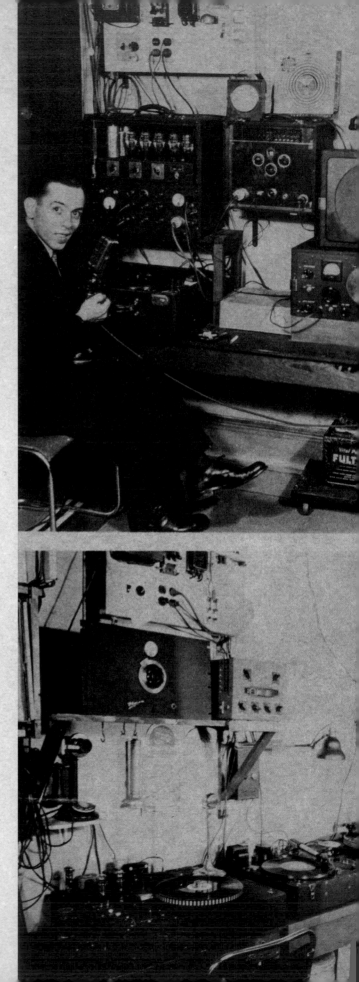

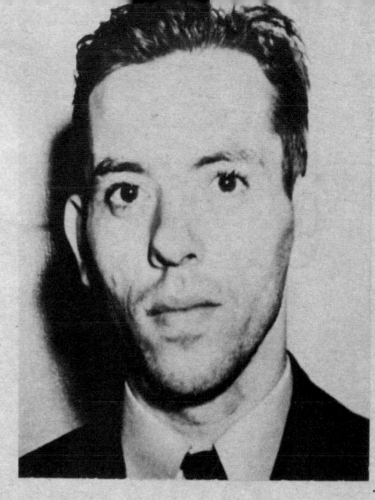

JOSEF KLEIN

This German spy ring "office"—and all its communications—was secretly monitored by the FBI in New York.

IN HONOR OF T
OF THE CENTRAL IN
WHO GAVE THEIR LIVES IN TH

8

A special memorial wall stands in the original headquarters of the Central Intelligence Agency (CIA) near Washington, D.C. As of 2012, it contained 102 black stars chiseled into white marble, each star representing a CIA agent who died while providing vital intelligence to the United States. A memorial book sits in a case below the stars. Sixty-two names are inscribed in the Book of Honor. No names are listed for the other 40 stars because these agents' identities must still remain a secret. Espionage has a long and proud history in the U.S. The memorial wall honors that tradition and also illustrates how dangerous the life of a spy can be.

SPIES IN WAR, SPIES IN PEACE

Long ago, Chinese soldier and philosopher Sun Tzu wrote, "All warfare is based on deception." By this he meant that a nation can't win a war without deceiving its enemies in some way or without uncovering information its enemies don't want revealed. As such, spying has been an important part of warfare throughout human history.

George Washington, America's first great military leader, probably agreed with Sun Tzu. One of his first acts as general of the Continental Army was to send an agent undercover to Boston to learn what the British army was planning there. Washington used many spies during the American Revolutionary War, and the information they provided helped turn the tide in several key battles. Some gathered intelligence about British strength and plans; others provided disinformation to fool the British. For example, in 1775, Washington discovered that his army based near Boston had only 36 barrels of gunpowder. Those would be used up quickly if

the British attacked. So the general sent agents into the city to spread the word that the Continental Army had 1,800 barrels on hand. The trick kept the British from advancing long enough for more powder to be brought in.

Spying by Americans was taken to new technological heights during the Civil War (1861–65). Alexander Gardner, one of America's first photographers, used his camera to spy for the Union, or the North. His pictures of Confederate (Southern) forces helped Union leaders uncover possible spies or double agents. The Union even used aerial reconnaissance by

sending spies above battlefields in Virginia in hydrogen-filled balloons equipped with telegraph equipment to report on Confederate troop movements.

The first official American intelligence agency was created in 1908, when the Justice Department established the Bureau of Information. In 1935, it was renamed the Federal Bureau of Investigation (FBI). The FBI is still the nation's main weapon against counterespionage within the U.S.

As the world began moving toward another war in the 1930s, the Signal Intelligence Service

Right: General Washington fearlessly led the Continental Army through eight years of war.

EVOLUTION OF ESPIONAGE
Harriet Tubman, Spy

Former slave Harriet Tubman is famous for the number of slaves she led to freedom via the Underground Railroad both before and during the Civil War. Many people may not realize that she also served as a Union spy. In 1862, the governor of Massachusetts sent her to South Carolina. Assuming the cover of a teacher and nurse to the African American Gullah people of the Sea Islands, Tubman organized a network of spies and scouts to gather intelligence behind Confederate lines. In the summer of 1863, Tubman helped lead a raiding party of more than 500 black soldiers that destroyed bridges and railroads and disrupted Confederate supply lines.

(SIS) was established to intercept and read communications sent by radio, telegraph, or telephone between Germany or Japan and their allies. This work often required deciphering intricate codes used to keep these messages secret. SIS agents achieved a major feat in 1940 by breaking the code used by Japanese government officials. They even intercepted a message just before December 7, 1941, revealing that Japan intended to attack the American naval base at Pearl Harbor, Hawaii. Unfortunately, a breakdown in communications delayed sending out an alert before the actual attack began. After the U.S. entered World War II (1939–45), the SIS greatly expanded its staff, going from 331 employees in 1941 to more than 10,000 by 1945.

The SIS played an important role after 1945 as the U.S. and Soviet Union entered the Cold War (1945–91). American leaders hoped to gather as much information as possible about the Soviet Union's plans as it expanded its communist hold over countries in Eastern Europe. The SIS evolved into a new organization in 1952, the National Security Agency (NSA). The NSA is now the country's largest intelligence agency, employing as many as 30,000 people. NSA experts analyze 50 to 100 million

Above: Born into slavery in Maryland, Harriet Tubman escaped when she was almost 30.

communications each year. Since the terrorist attacks against the U.S. on September 11, 2001, the NSA's powers have expanded to include monitoring telephone calls and e-mails sent to and from suspected terrorists in the U.S.

While the SIS kept busy during World War II deciphering coded enemy messages, the FBI was focused on uncovering spy operations within the U.S. A number of pro-German and pro-Japanese spy rings were broken up, often with the help of moles or double agents. The FBI took on another key mission during the Cold War: identifying Americans spying for the Soviets.

In 1942, an entirely new intelligence agency was born—the Office of Strategic Services (OSS). Organized by William "Wild Bill" Donovan, a World

SIS members in the mid-1930s were tasked with outwitting America's enemies overseas.

Julia Child's bright personality made her a favorite TV chef—and an unsuspected spy.

War I (1914–18) combat hero and intelligence expert, the OSS carried out covert operations to support the U.S. and its allies during World War II. Donovan's nickname was fitting; he was always coming up with wild ideas. Once, he even proposed using bats to drop firebombs on Japan! Under Donovan's direction, OSS agents landed behind enemy lines to gather intelligence needed by army and navy units. They also smuggled supplies to resistance groups and recruited German and Japanese citizens to spy on their own countries.

Above: John Ford was head of the photographic unit for the OSS and made films for the Navy.

After the war ended in 1945, U.S. president Harry Truman wanted to disband the OSS. However, Donovan changed Truman's mind by outlining the threats posed by the emerging power of the Soviet Union. In 1947, the OSS was renamed the CIA. The independent agency reports directly to the president and has become the principal American intelligence agency acting outside the country. Most people in Washington simply call it "The Company."

The CIA's main objectives are to support governments and leaders who, like the U.S., oppose communism and terrorism and to undermine governments that may pose a threat to American interests and security. The CIA carries out

EVOLUTION OF ESPIONAGE
OSS All-Stars

Wild Bill Donovan brought together an unusual group of spies in the OSS. He recruited educated men and women and challenged them to find creative ways of undermining the Germans and Japanese. Among those recruited were Hollywood directors John Ford and Merian Cooper, future culinary expert Julia Child, and major-league baseball catcher Moe Berg. Ford and Cooper made documentaries and propaganda films. Child helped develop a shark repellent used by OSS divers attempting to sabotage German submarines. Berg, who could speak seven languages, was sent abroad to Latin America and Europe to scope out atomic secrets and assess the loyalties of foreign leaders.

its work through four divisions: (1) the National Clandestine Service, or NCS (spies operating in the field); (2) the Directorate of Science and Technology (creators of special gadgets used by spies and instruments such as satellites, spy planes, cameras, and bugs used to obtain information); (3) the Directorate of Intelligence (information analysts); and (4) the Directorate of Support (those responsible for training, supplies, and security, including such tasks as weeding out moles and double agents working inside the CIA itself). Of the Company's approximately 20,000 employees, only about 10 percent are spies.

While most of its employees live and work near the agency's headquarters in the Washington suburb of Langley, Virginia, the NCS maintains stations in 130 other countries. Some stations have only 1 operative; others have as many as 50. Their job is to analyze political and military developments in their countries, recruit local people to provide intelligence, and determine if covert action needs to be taken to protect American interests. Operating in secrecy, CIA agents seldom receive recognition for their accomplishments, but they do sometimes get criticized for acting recklessly or breaking other countries' laws.

EVOLUTION OF ESPIONAGE
The Zimmermann Telegram

By early 1917, the U.S. had still not entered World War I. Then German submarines began attacking any nation's ships that sailed into British ports. The U.S. responded by breaking diplomatic ties with Germany. Anticipating this development, German foreign minister Arthur Zimmermann had sent a coded telegram to his ambassadors in Washington and Mexico City. The message offered Mexico territory in the U.S. if it joined with Germany against the Americans. British cryptographers broke the code and sent a copy to American intelligence leaders in February 1917. The message was printed in newspapers across the country, and, within weeks, the U.S. declared war on Germany.

Arthur Zimmermann resigned from his post six months after he sent the infamous telegram.

SPIES AND MICE

The spies you see on television and in the movies lead glamorous lives, wear cool disguises, and are usually attractive. Think of Jason Bourne of the *Bourne* trilogy, Jack Bauer of *24*, or Sydney Bristow of *Alias*. In real life, espionage agencies such as the CIA recruit average-looking people who can blend in with others around them. In spy talk, the ability to blend in is called "going gray." Gray doesn't stand out the way bright colors do.

Despite what you see in movies, only a small percentage of CIA operatives actually do undercover spy work themselves. Some operatives working undercover really do use top-secret tools and weapons to collect information or to carry out covert actions against foreigners who pose a threat to America. Most CIA agents, however, spend their time recruiting others in their station areas to gather intelligence for the U.S. They take on the role of handler.

To survive in the field, a CIA agent needs a good legend, or cover story. The legend answers the questions *Who am I?* and *What am I doing here?* Some CIA operatives work under their own names. In spy talk, they are legals—they do their spying while officially working in the American embassy in a foreign country. As American government employees, they can bend some rules of the foreign country without fear of being arrested. If they are caught breaking the law, they are usually sent back to the U.S. rather than jailed.

Other CIA spies are classified as illegals—they do their spying using a false name and a made-up identity. If their cover is blown, the U.S. government will probably deny any knowledge of them or their mission. (You know about such denial if you have seen any of the *Mission: Impossible* movies or television episodes.) If they are caught, their punishment is often severe and might include torture or execution. Some CIA illegals are probably represented by stars on the agency's memorial wall.

What makes people want to be spies—or agree to become spies, even against their will? According to American journalist and espionage expert Ernest Volkman, the reasons can be summed up using the

Opposite: Matt Damon played Jason Bourne in the first three movies, including 2004's *The Bourne Supremacy.*

EVOLUTION OF ESPIONAGE
The Hollow Nickel

In 1953, newspaper delivery boy Jimmy Bozart was paid with a nickel that seemed lighter than normal. When he dropped the coin, it split in two, revealing a photograph of a coded message inside. Bozart gave the coin and photo to the police, who then passed them on to the FBI, and they remained a mystery for nearly four years. Then a Soviet spy named Reino Hayhanen defected in May 1957. He provided the FBI with a code book and information about a spy ring operating in the U.S. under the leadership of Rudolf Abel. Abel was soon arrested and tried for espionage. Later, he was swapped for downed American U-2 pilot Francis Gary Powers.

acronym MICE. The letters represent the words *money*, *ideology*, *compromise*, and *ego*. Some people become spies because they are paid well for the information they uncover and transmit. Others become spies because they have a strong belief in their country or in the ideals represented by another country. Others may be compromised, or blackmailed, into spying to avoid punishment or to prevent some dark secret about themselves from being revealed. Still others may think that becoming a spy is the way to show off how clever or daring they can be.

The famous American traitor Benedict Arnold spied for the British in the Revolutionary War for money and also because his ego was hurt when he was passed over for Continental Army promotions he felt he deserved.

American communists Julius and Ethel Rosenberg were executed as traitors in 1953 for revealing American secrets about the atomic bomb to the Soviet Union. They acted because of their strong belief in communist ideology.

People who want to become CIA agents don't simply complete an application, undergo classroom and on-the-job-training, and then get sent undercover to a foreign country. It is a long and complicated process. According to the CIA's own Web site (www.cia.gov), the Company looks for individuals who can deal with "fast-moving, ambiguous, and unstructured situations." In other words, the CIA wants people who can think on their feet and not get flustered when things go wrong—and things often do go wrong. The Web

Above: Benedict Arnold fled after his plot to surrender an American fort to the British backfired.

DAILY NEWS 3¢

Copr. 1951 by News Syndicate Co. Inc. **NEW YORK'S** PICTURE NEWSPAPER Trade Mark Reg. U. S. Pat. Off.

Vol. 32. No. 245   New York 17, Friday, April 6, 1951★   88 Main+4 Manhattan Pages   3 Cents IN CITY LIMITS | 4 CENTS in Suburbs | 5 CENTS Elsewhere

A-SPY COUPLE DOOMED TO DIE

—Story on Page 3

Use Chiang's Army, Mac Asks

—Story on Page 2

On Way to Chair. Gloved hands folded, Mrs. Ethel Rosenberg, 35, rides in rear of prison van on way to Women's House of Detention. Julius Rosenberg, 32, is separated from his wife by wire screen in van outside U. S. Courthouse. They were sentenced to death for passing A-bomb secrets to Reds, enabling Russia to perfect bomb ahead of schedule. —Story p. 3

(NEWS foto by Bill Meurer)

Below: In the 1930s, polygraph exams were a relatively new form of testing a person's truthfulness.

site adds, "This requires physical and psychological health, energy, intuition, 'street sense,' and the ability to cope with stress."

The CIA puts its applicants through a series of tough tests— physical, mental, and medical exams; polygraph (lie-detector) tests; background checks; and writing tests (after all, most agents spend a lot of time writing reports). Of the 100 or so top recruits in a given class, only about 17 make it through the testing. Then the serious training begins.

What kind of training do CIA operatives receive? Former agent Lindsay Moran reveals some of the secrets in her 2005 book *Blowing My Cover* and in a series of online videos found on the Web site www.videojug.com. A fairly realistic view of the training is also presented in the 2003 movie *The Recruit*. Operative training takes place at Camp Peary, located near Williamsburg, Virginia. CIA agents call it "The Farm." The course at the Farm includes paramilitary training—martial arts and hand-to-hand combat, use of guns and knives, and field survival techniques. Potential agents learn to drive defensively, to handle speedboats, and to parachute from planes and helicopters. They also endure a "jail sequence," in which they are put

in a cell, deprived of food, water, and sleep, and then interrogated nonstop for nearly two days to test their mental toughness.

According to Moran, the physical training was both exciting and scary, but she seldom used what she practiced once she was in the field. Other training elements, called tradecraft, proved more useful. These tactics included learning how to develop a cover and how to improvise if the cover needs to change; how to spot a tail and avoid being followed; how to use spy cameras, radios and radio detecting devices, and other communication tools; how to mingle comfortably at parties and in the streets or set up secret meetings to recruit local assets; and how to set up a drop for collecting intelligence from assets. Moran says, "You are taught specifically how to spot people who might be potential recruits and how to assess their personality to determine whether or not they might be a good foreign spy. Also, how to seek out their weaknesses . . . that you can prey upon in order to convince them to spy on behalf of the United States." The entire process usually takes more than a year. Then recruits are ready to begin their careers as spies. There is only one catch: They can never tell anyone what they really do for a living.

TOOLS AND TRICKS

In spy movies, the heroes often travel on land in high-speed cars equipped with machine guns and rocket boosters, go airborne via jet packs or flying machines, or travel underwater in mini-submarines. They fire guns concealed in briefcases, cufflinks, or umbrellas; attack enemies with shoes armed with poison tips; make calls from a phone concealed in a shoe; and photograph meetings and documents using the tiniest cameras imaginable. Do real spy gadgets and weapons match those of the movies?

The answer is both yes and no. The CIA's Directorate of Science and Technology (DS&T) is responsible for developing or purchasing gadgets for the agency. Much of the DS&T's budget over the years has been invested in aerial reconnaissance—spy planes (manned and unmanned), satellites, and the long-range photographic equipment they carry. One of the latest spy plane models is the Global Hawk, which was first used in the War in Afghanistan in 2002. The Global Hawk is an unmanned drone that can fly 350 miles (563 km) per hour at altitudes of more

than 60,000 feet (18,288 m) for up to 30 hours straight. Equipped with high-speed cameras and infrared scanners, the Global Hawk can detect anything made of metal on the ground and has even spotted openings of caves in the mountains of Afghanistan that ground troops missed while searching the area on foot. You won't find James Bond piloting a Global Hawk, but these planes have proven effective in recognizing enemy military bases and tracking troop movements.

Over the years, U.S. spy planes have provided vital information but have caused some embarrassment for the country, too. In 1960, for example, a manned American aircraft called the U-2 was shot down while flying illegally within Soviet airspace. The pilot was eventually released as part of a spy exchange, but the plane was never returned.

Modern intelligence work, however, is not just "spy from the sky." Many other gadgets developed at Langley have been designed for use on the ground. These include subminiature cameras (using 16-mm film) for photographing secret documents or meetings; electronic listening equipment for eavesdropping, as well as

Today, unmanned Predator drones carry out reconnaissance and missile strikes around the world.

Fidel Castro's habit of smoking cigars led would-be assassins to target that object.

anti-bugging devices to protect Americans from enemy ears; radios and cipher machines to make sure that communications stay secret; guns hidden within gloves, cigarette packs, or fountain pens; and even poison darts. Some other unusual weapons fall into the "dirty tricks" category. For example, a CIA scientist once tried to develop cigars that would poison Cuban dictator Fidel Castro when he lit one up. The same scientist also formulated special chemicals that, when placed in Castro's boots, would make his hair fall out and embarrass him. Nothing came of these plans, though.

A number of the gadgets and weapons developed by the DS&T have been controversial—explosives, poisons, nerve gases, chemicals that destroy crops, drugs used as truth serums, and so on. Not everyone agrees that such weaponry is fair to use, even in defending the U.S. against terrorists. For that reason, some have never been used outside the laboratory.

The types of gadgets and techniques used by American spies have changed over time. For most of history, collecting secret

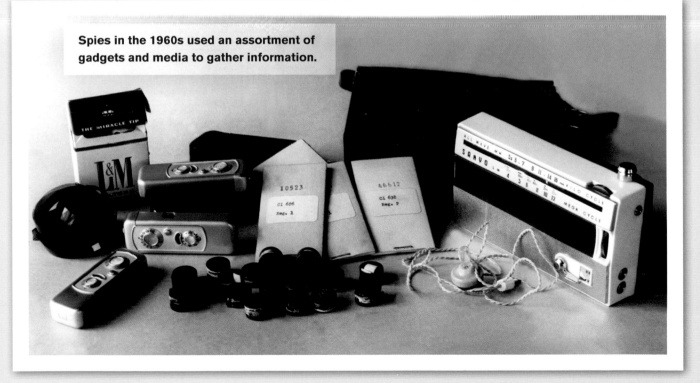

Spies in the 1960s used an assortment of gadgets and media to gather information.

information was done directly by individuals using deception and trickery and a few relatively simple tools. In spy language, this is called HUMINT (human intelligence). A spy involved in HUMINT will usually have several of these tools on hand: a code book for encoding or decoding messages; a disguise kit containing sunglasses, hair dye, wigs, and hats; a lock pick gun or break-in kit; night-vision goggles to see in the dark; a miniature camera to photograph documents and equipment to convert those photos into microdots; and both listening and radio broadcasting equipment.

Perhaps surprisingly, many agents don't carry guns or knives during their day-to-day spy work. Oleg Kalugin, who spied for the Soviet Union in the U.S. for many years, said, "We never carried weapons in our foreign assignments. Our weapons were our training, our intelligence, and our understanding of what was going on." Kalugin added that, if any tools were needed, he was far more likely to use a camera or miniature bugging device than a gun.

Starting in the 20th century, spies began using various types of technology to help them obtain information—from new cameras to hidden microphones to radio waves to computers. For example,

the CIA, NSA, and other spy agencies gather ELINT (electronic intelligence) via the Internet and through computer monitoring or hacking; COMINT (communication intelligence) by intercepting radio, telephone, and other communications; and PHOTINT (photographic intelligence) by studying photographs taken by spy planes, satellites, or human operatives. All of these new methods fall under the heading of TECHINT (technical intelligence). This means that modern spies need a wide range of technical skills and support. Learning to use high-tech gadgets has become an important part of their tradecraft.

Today, it is probably more important for an American spy to know how to operate or hack into a computer than how to engage in hand-to-hand combat. Computers can be bugged with a keystroke recorder that can help an agent determine a user's password and duplicate any commands that were previously typed in. Other software, or programs, can be installed to enable an agent to download files for later analysis. With so much information stored digitally these days, it is becoming harder than ever to keep a secret.

In recent years, the CIA has also found ways to use computers as

OXIDIZER TRAILER

6 MISSILE TRANSPORTERS

ERECTOR

3 MISSILE TRANSPORTERS

Reliable PHOTINT can be invaluable to an agency or government during national crises or conflicts.

Thanks to CIA intelligence, the U.S. Army was able to operate effectively during the Gulf War.

weapons. For example, during the Gulf War in the early 1990s, CIA computer experts played a trick on Iraqi president Saddam Hussein and his generals. Even before the war began in January 1991, they programmed a virus—a program that can take over a computer—into a chip built into a printer. A CIA mole working inside Iraq's air-defense headquarters in the city of Baghdad hooked up the printer. When the war broke out, a signal was sent to activate the virus, which shut down the defense system in less than a minute. By the time the virus was controlled, many of Iraq's aircraft had been destroyed by United Nations (UN) troops. The CIA also used the Internet to spread false information about UN troop movements during the war, misleading Iraqi military leaders.

Below: The NSA includes signals intelligence (SIGINT) in its methods of gathering global TECHINT.

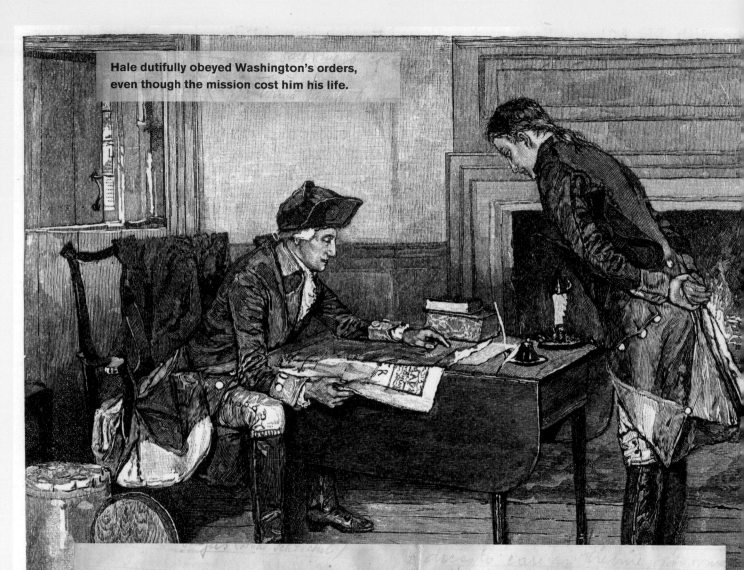

Hale dutifully obeyed Washington's orders, even though the mission cost him his life.

EVOLUTION OF ESPIONAGE
Revolutionary Secrets

The Culper Spy Ring often used a special ink called "Jay's Sympathetic Stain" to write secret messages to George Washington during the Revolutionary War. The ink would disappear as it dried and reappear when brushed with a second liquid. The spies wrote their invisible ink messages between the lines of ordinary letters. In one 1780 message, spies reported movement of British troops to Newport, Rhode Island, to attack French reinforcements. As a trick, Washington wrote a letter describing plans for a major attack on enemy troops in New York and had a double agent pass it along to the British. The "redcoats" returned to New York, allowing the French to land safely.

SPECIAL SPIES

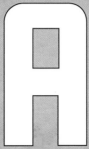

America's first famous spy, Nathan Hale, was one of its least successful. After the U.S. lost several early Revolutionary battles to the British near New York in 1776, Hale, a 21-year-old army captain from Connecticut, agreed to go behind enemy lines to learn where the British army planned to attack next. Posing as a Dutch schoolteacher, Hale talked with British troops and Loyalists in New York, jotting down notes that he hid inside his shoes. After a week of fact-finding, Hale stood on a dock in New York awaiting a boat that would take him back to the American side. Unfortunately, a British boat arrived first, and Hale was captured and questioned. When his hidden notes were discovered, Hale confessed that he was a Continental Army officer posing as a civilian. British General William Howe ordered that no mercy be shown to this spy, and Hale was hanged the next morning without a trial. According to legend, Hale's last words were, "I only regret that I have but one life to lose for my country."

Hale's classmate at Yale College, Benjamin Tallmadge, was more successful. He led a group of American spies in the New York area known as the Culper Spy Ring. This group pioneered several unusual methods for transmitting the information its members gathered, including invisible ink and a number substitution cipher, in which numbers stand for letters. The ring also arranged a special signal when messages were ready for pickup. One member of the group, Anna Strong, would hang a black undergarment on her clothesline and a pattern of handkerchiefs to indicate in which cove on Long Island a spy was waiting. A boat would then sail in to the specified cove, pick up the coded messages, and take them to Tallmadge for delivery to General Washington.

Spies played an important role during the Civil War for both the North and South. Several of the most successful spies were women, who seemed able to engage army leaders in conversation and learn secret information without rousing suspicion. Rose Greenhow, a beautiful widow who lived in Washington, D.C., is sometimes credited with helping the Confederacy win the Battle of Bull

As the Germans marched across Europe in the 1940s (below), they used code machines (opposite) to transmit messages.

Run in July 1861. Greenhow often hosted parties that Union officers attended. At one party she learned that the Union intended to attack at Bull Run six days later. She wrote out a 10-word message, using a code in which symbols represented the letters of the alphabet, and had a friend carry the message to Confederate General P. G. T. Beauregard. The general was then able to prepare for the attack and win the battle.

Fast-forward to the 20th century. Two other important figures in American intelligence history emerged during and after World War I—Herbert Yardley and William Friedman. They didn't gather or transmit secret information; rather, they uncovered secrets using cryptography. Both men were scientific geniuses and had an uncanny ability to detect patterns in coded messages. They were part of a government organization known as the American Black Chamber that assisted the U.S. State Department and military intelligence with code and cipher work. Yardley was an expert on word and book codes, while Friedman specialized in breaking rotor codes, in which a series of rotors containing letters and numbers generates millions of code possibilities. Both men had a special focus on Japanese codes in the years before World War II began, and Friedman's team cracked the Japanese military code nicknamed "Purple." Having the ability to decipher messages composed in Purple code likely saved thousands of American lives during World War II.

One of the most accomplished OSS agents of the 1940s was Virginia Hall, who was called the "Limping Lady of the OSS" because she had an artificial leg. Hall spoke perfect French and went undercover in German-occupied

France in 1940. She had a warm, motherly style, and many lonely German soldiers stationed in France confided in her. In addition to passing along information she learned from these soldiers, Hall also helped stranded Allied pilots escape from France. When the Germans began to suspect her, Hall made a long and difficult journey by foot into Spain and then back to a new location in France, where she set up a radio to report on German troop movements and arrange for food and supply drops. After the war, President Truman wanted to honor her with the Distinguished Service Cross. Hall said she would accept the medal only if it was presented to her in private because she wanted to

remain undercover as a member of what would become the CIA.

During the Cold War, spying and counterintelligence efforts intensified. On the American side were the CIA, FBI, and NSA; on the Soviet side was the KGB. Both nations put many operatives in the field, recruited assets or moles to spy in their own countries, and did what they could to bribe or turn agents to become double agents.

One of the most significant Cold War double agents was high-ranking KGB officer Oleg Penkovsky. In August 1960, worried that Soviet leader Nikita Khrushchev was going to lead the world into a nuclear war, Penkovsky passed a message to two American tourists on a Moscow bridge and

EVOLUTION OF ESPIONAGE
Failure in the Sky

In the mid-1950s, the CIA decided that its agents on the ground could not effectively monitor the growing nuclear capabilities of the Soviet Union. So the agency commissioned construction of the U-2 spy plane, which could fly high enough to avoid detection or attack. In May 1960, U-2 pilot Francis Gary Powers was taking photographs over Soviet territory when an engine failed. The plane dropped to a vulnerable altitude and was struck by Soviet missiles. Powers was thrown from the plane before he could set it to self-destruct. He was captured and tried for espionage in a public trial designed to embarrass the U.S.

Developed for the CIA in the mid-1950s, the U-2 is now operated by U.S. Air Force pilots.

asked them to get it to the CIA. In the message, Penkovsky offered to provide information to American and British intelligence. Over the next two years, Penkovsky hid messages inside candy boxes or placed them into drops, giving the U.S. and Britain important details about Soviet missile strength and capabilities. Using this information, U.S. president John F. Kennedy was able to confront the Soviets in October 1962 when they were installing missiles in a military headquarters they had established in Cuba. The Soviets backed down, and a war was averted. However, Penkovsky was arrested in Moscow and later executed as a traitor.

Who are America's super spies of the 21st century? In most cases, they must remain anonymous, and their efforts stay cloaked in secrecy. Whether they are trying to uncover or undermine terrorists in countries such as Afghanistan, Pakistan, Iraq, or Iran or working to help the U.S. deal with communist governments in the Americas, their missions are vital to American security.

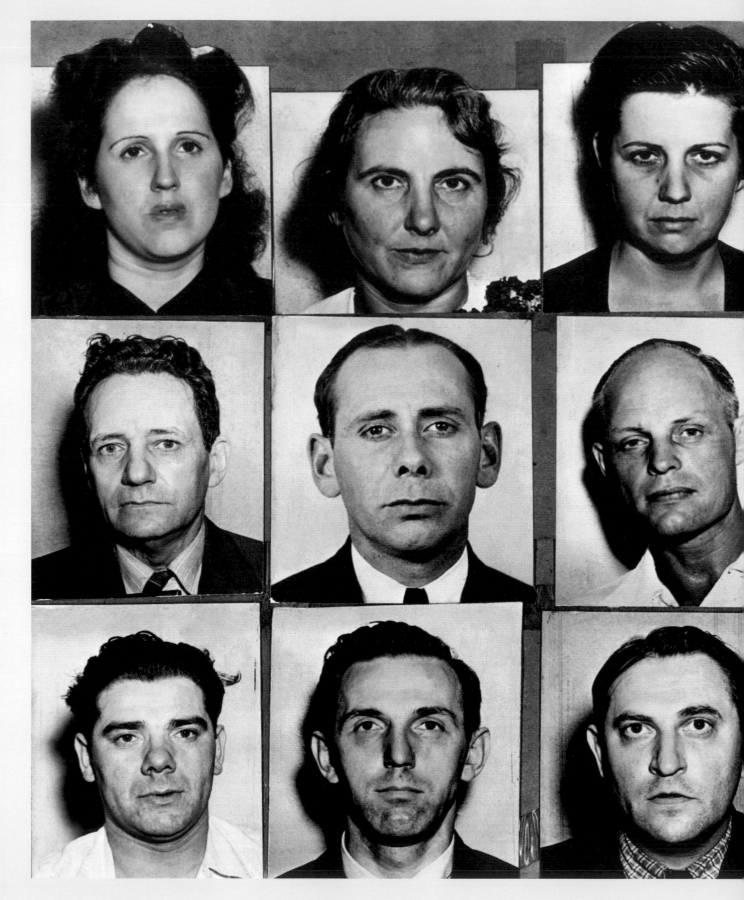

ON A MISSION

Throughout the 20th century and into the 21st, U.S. intelligence agencies have been actively involved in covert activities directed against America's enemies. Some of their spying activities have been as exciting as Hollywood movies, and a few have even been made into films. Some of the missions have ended successfully and added to American security. Others have ended unsuccessfully and led to embarrassing situations for the country.

One successful FBI mission during the early days of World War II was dramatic enough to be made into a 1945 movie called *The House on 92nd Street*. It started in September 1939, when an American aircraft factory manager named William Sebold was visiting relatives in Germany. Members of the Gestapo, the German secret police, approached Sebold about joining a German spy ring in New York City led by Frederick Duquesne. He was expected to send reports on American defense plans to Germany. Instead, Sebold offered to help the FBI break up the Duquesne Spy Ring.

Sebold received training from the Gestapo on how to set up a radio and transmit messages to Germany using secret codes. He passed these codes along to the FBI. With the FBI's help, Sebold also set up an office in New York where his meetings with members of the German spy ring were secretly filmed. Over the next 16 months, Sebold sent and received hundreds of messages that were intercepted and often altered by the FBI so as to provide nothing useful to Germany. In 1941, the FBI ended its counterespionage operation by convicting 33 Duquesne Ring members on counts of espionage and other charges.

Following World War II, American intelligence agencies turned to dealing with the rise of communism around the world. The CIA's Cold War-era operations were designed to help overthrow communist-leaning governments and place in power governments that would be more supportive of U.S. political and business interests. In 1947, for example, CIA operatives used money and propaganda to stop the Italian Communist Party from winning national elections. In 1954, CIA

Opposite: Frederick Duquesne (middle row, far left) and eight members of his ring are shown in mug shots.

agents provided assistance to military leaders in Guatemala to overthrow its pro-communist president.

The most controversial CIA operations were those carried out in the powerful, oil-producing country of Iran. In 1953, the shah, or king, of Iran was pushed out of power, and a newly elected government took over. British and American oil companies had major wells and plants in Iran, and the new prime minister threatened to nationalize these. Western leaders worried that Iran might cut off oil to Britain and the U.S. or raise prices significantly. The CIA supported the efforts of Iranians who overthrew the new government and brought the shah back to power. Over the next 25 years, the shah ruled with an iron hand, often oppressing his people. Still, CIA advisers continued to train the shah's secret police to help him hold power. Then, in 1979, these secret police turned on the shah. A new government took over, led by a radical Muslim religious leader known as the Ayatollah Khomeini. Since that time, the Iranian and American governments have often clashed.

Starting in 1959, the CIA began to focus on a new problem—a communist dictatorship established by Fidel Castro 90 miles (145 km) from Florida on the island of Cuba. Many Cubans who opposed Castro

A Bad Year for Spies

In one year, 1985, four high-profile arrests were made of Americans spying for other countries. Hungry for money, U.S. Navy communications specialist John Walker had been spying for the Soviets since the 1960s and had recruited his friend, brother, and son into his ring. Jewish naval intelligence officer Jonathan Pollard was arrested for revealing U.S. military secrets to Israel. Retired CIA translator Larry Wu Tai Chin was charged with providing information that had led to the deaths of many spies working for the U.S. in China, while former NSA employee Ronald Pelton—who had a photographic memory—was charged with providing military secrets to the Soviets.

Although Shah Pahlavi regained control of Iran in 1953, he was to lose it again in 1979.

Above: The CIA-trained Cubans who survived the Bay of Pigs attack were imprisoned for 22 months afterward.

fled to the U.S. and began making plans to overthrow the dictator and reestablish a democracy in their homeland. The CIA was eager to support Cubans in their efforts to topple Castro. So, in April 1961, an attack force of 1,500 Cubans with CIA help sailed from Nicaragua to the Bay of Pigs in southern Cuba, where they planned to land and start a revolution. Unfortunately, Castro had been warned about the attack, and his air force and ground troops wiped out the invaders, capturing nearly 1,200 and killing another 100. The U.S. government was forced to negotiate with Castro for the release of the rebels and eventually agreed to pay $53 million in food and supplies.

One of the most unusual CIA Cold War missions did not involve toppling governments or even going undercover. It was organized to learn Soviet nuclear secrets hidden more than three miles (4.8 km) beneath the sea. In April 1968, an explosion occurred in a Soviet nuclear submarine sailing approximately 750 miles (1,207 km) northwest of Hawaii. The sub quickly sank to the ocean floor. U.S. Navy underwater microphones picked up the explosion and pinpointed the sub's location. But how could they recover the sub and find the nuclear weapons and secret coding information they believed it contained?

Four years later, the CIA came up with a plan to raise the sub and uncover its secrets. The CIA teamed with billionaire Hollywood movie producer and aviation pioneer Howard Hughes to build a $200-million salvage ship called the *Glomar Explorer*. In July 1974, the *Glomar Explorer* reached the spot where the submarine lay, and a giant clawlike device was lowered to grab it. Suddenly, the claw snapped, and part of the submarine broke off. The rest was pulled up successfully. Inside were found three nuclear missiles, two nuclear torpedoes, the ship's code machine, and various code books. The recovered section

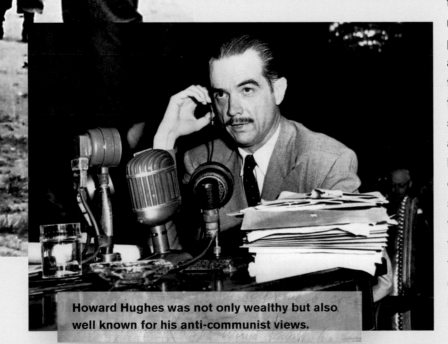

Howard Hughes was not only wealthy but also well known for his anti-communist views.

43

EVOLUTION OF ESPIONAGE
The Hunt Ends

For nine years following "9/11," Osama bin Laden, the mastermind behind the attacks, dodged discovery by the CIA. Then, in the fall of 2010, CIA agents in Pakistan located bin Laden's likely hiding place near the city of Abbottabad. They observed the building carefully for many months, just to be certain. Then, on May 1, 2011, U.S. president Barack Obama gave the go-ahead for an attack. In a daring 40-minute raid early in the morning of May 2, a team of Navy SEALs broke into the building, found bin Laden, killed him, gathered vital papers and tapes stored in his room, and quickly flew out of Pakistan, their mission successfully accomplished.

also contained the bloated bodies of eight Soviet sailors who were buried at sea in a solemn ceremony.

Terrorist activities in the 1990s and 2000s have caused the American intelligence community to act with new focus, both inside and outside the country. For example, after a federal office building in Oklahoma City was bombed in April 1995, the FBI conducted the largest criminal investigation in U.S. history. Within days of the bombing, two former American soldiers were arrested. They were later convicted of the crime in which 168 people died and 324 buildings were destroyed or damaged.

Following the attacks on the World Trade Center in New York and the Pentagon near Washington, D.C., on September 11, 2001, president George W. Bush declared a war on terrorism and called for all American intelligence agencies to better coordinate their efforts to uncover and halt terrorist plots. Working together, American intelligence agencies are today helping the U.S. battle terrorism and other threats in 130 countries on 6 different continents. In this way, spies are protecting Americans every day.

Opposite: After being struck by airplanes on 9/11, the twin towers of the World Trade Center collapsed.

ENDNOTES

aerial reconnaissance—spying activities conducted through the air using airplanes, balloons, and drones

agent—a person who works for, but is not necessarily officially employed by, an intelligence service

Allied—relating to the side in World War II that included the United States, Great Britain, France, and the Soviet Union

assets—hidden sources acting as spies or providing secret information to a spy

bugs—electronic listening devices that usually contain a microphone, transmitter, and antenna

Cold War—the hostile competition between the United States and its allies against the Soviet Union and its allies that began at the end of World War II and lasted until the collapse of the Soviet Union in 1991

communist—describing a political and economic system in which all goods and property are owned by the state and shared by all members of the public

counterespionage—efforts made by a nation's intelligence agency to catch and eliminate spies working against the country and protect the country against sabotage or terrorism

covert operations—undercover or hidden activities

cryptographers—people who practice the art of writing and deciphering messages in code

deciphering—breaking secret codes, or ciphers, often used to send spy communications

defected—in the context of spying, chose to leave the control of one country's intelligence service to work for another country; defectors often provide vital information to their new country

disinformation—false or misleading intelligence, often provided by double agents

double agents—spies for one country who double as spies for a second country and often provide false information to the first country

drone—an unmanned aircraft, often directed by remote control, that is used to take secret photographs of or attack targets

drop—a secure location that usually includes a sealed container where spies and their handlers can exchange information or intelligence materials to avoid meeting in person

embassy—the headquarters of an ambassador and staff in a foreign country

handler—a case officer who is responsible for recruiting and directing agents and assets working in a country

infrared—light rays used in photography or night vision equipment; infrared rays show changes in heat

intelligence—information uncovered and transmitted by a spy

moles—employees of one intelligence service who actually work for another service or who work undercover in a foreign country in order to supply intelligence

nationalize—to transfer private ownership or control of resources or industries to the national government

operative—an undercover agent working for an intelligence agency

propaganda—material distributed to promote a government's or group's point of view or to damage an opposing point of view; some propaganda is untrue or unfairly exaggerated

resistance groups—organized underground movements in a country fighting against a foreign power that is occupying the country

tail—someone following a spy who is acting undercover

tradecraft—the procedures, techniques, and devices used by spies to carry out their activities

WEB SITES

CIA Personality Quiz
https://www.cia.gov/careers/cia-personality-quiz.html
Take a quiz and learn more about what the CIA is—and is not.

National Cryptologic Museum
http://www.nsa.gov/about/cryptologic_heritage/museum/index.shtml
Find out more about America's history of cryptology and take a virtual tour.

SELECTED BIBLIOGRAPHY

Bamford, James. *Body of Secrets: Anatomy of the Ultra-Secret National Security Agency: from the Cold War through the Dawn of a New Century*. New York: Doubleday, 2001.

Coleman, Janet Wyman. *Secrets, Lies, Gizmos, and Spies: A History of Spies and Espionage*. New York: Abrams Books for Young Readers, 2006.

Crowdy, Terry. *The Enemy Within: A History of Espionage*. Oxford: Osprey Publishing, 2006.

Hastedt, Glenn. *Espionage: A Reference Handbook*. Santa Barbara, Calif., 2003.

Moran, Lindsay. *Blowing My Cover: My Life as a CIA Spy*. New York: G. P. Putnam, 2005.

Owen, David. *Spies: The Undercover World of Secrets, Gadgets, and Lies*. Buffalo, N.Y.: Firefly Books, 2004.

Priest, Dana, and William M. Arkin. "Top Secret America: A Washington Post Investigation: Monitoring America." *The Washington Post*, July 19–21, 2010. http://projects.washingtonpost.com/top-secret-america/articles.

Volkman, Ernest. *Spies: The Secret Agents Who Changed the Course of History*. New York: John Wiley & Sons, 1994.

INDEX